PURSUIT

Start Publishing PD LLC
Copyright © 2024 by Start Publishing PD LLC

All rights reserved, including the right to reproduce this book or portions thereof in any form whatsoever.

Start Publishing PD is a registered trademark of Start Publishing PD LLC
Manufactured in the United States of America

Cover art: Shutterstock/Taisiya Kozorez

Cover design: Jennifer Do

10 9 8 7 6 5 4 3 2 1

ISBN 979-8-8809-1037-3

PURSUIT

by Lester del Rey

I

Fear cut through the unconscious mind of Wilbur Hawkes. With almost physical violence, it tightened his throat and knifed at his heart. It darted into his numbed brain, screaming at him.

He was a soft egg in a vast globe of elastic gelatine. Two creatures swam menacingly through the resisting globe toward him. The gelatine fought against them, but they came on. One was near, and made a mystic pass. He screamed at it, and the gelatine grew stronger, throwing them back and away. Suddenly, the creatures drew back. A door opened, and they were gone. But he couldn't let them go. If they escaped....

Hawkes jerked upright in his bed, gasping out a hoarse cry, and the sound of his own voice completed the awakening. He opened his eyes to a murky darkness that was barely relieved by the little night-light. For a second, the nightmare was so strong on his mind that he seemed to see two shadows beyond the door, rushing down the steps. He fought off the illusion, and with straining senses jerked his head around the room. There was nothing there.

Sweat was beading his forehead, and he could feel his pulse racing. He had to get out—had to leave—at once!

He forced the idea aside. There was something cloudy in his mind, but he made reason take over and shove away some of the heavy fear. His fingers found a cigarette and lighted it automatically. The first familiar breath of smoke in his lungs helped. He drew in deeply again, while the tiny sounds in the room became meaningful. There was the insistent ticking of a clock and the soft shushing sound of a tape recorder. He stared at the machine, running on fast rewind, and reversed it to play. But the tape seemed to be blank, or erased.

He crushed the cigarette out on a table-top where other butts lay in disorder. It looked wrong, and his mind leaped up in sudden frantic fear, before he could calm it again. This time, reason echoed his emotional unease.

PURSUIT

Hawkes had never smoked before!

But his fingers were already lighting another by old habit. His thoughts lurched, seeking for an answer. There was only a vague sense of something missing—a period of time seemed to have passed. It felt like a long period, but he had no memory of it. There had been the final fight with Irma, when he'd gone stalking out of the house, telling her to get a divorce any way she wanted. He'd opened the mail-box and taken out a letter—a letter from a Professor....

His mind refused to go further. There was only a complete blank after that. But it had been in midwinter, and now he could make out the faint outlines of full-leafed trees against the sky through the window! Months had gone by—and there was no faintest trace of them in his mind.

They'll get you! You can't escape! Hurry, go, GO!...

The cigarette fell from his shaking hands, and he was half out of the bed before the rational part of his mind could cut off the fear thoughts. He flipped on the lights, afraid of the dimness. It didn't help. The room was dusty, as if unused for months, and there was a cobweb in one corner by the mirror.

His own face shocked him. It was the same lean, sharp-featured face as ever, under the shock of nondescript, sandy hair. His ears still stuck out too much, and his lips were a trifle too thin. It looked no more than his thirty years; but it was a strained face, now—painted with weeks of fatigue, and grayish with fear, sweat-streaked and with nervous tension in every corded tendon of his throat. His somewhat bony, average-height figure shook visibly as he climbed from the bed.

Hawkes stood fighting himself, trying to get back in the bed, but it was a losing battle. Something seemed to swing up in the corner of the room, as if a shadow moved. He jerked his head toward it, but there was nothing there.

He heard his breath gasping harshly, and his knuckles whitened. There was the taste of blood in the corner of his mouth where he was biting his lips.

LESTER DEL REY

Get out! They'll be here at once! Leave—GO!

*

His hands were already fumbling with his under-clothing. He drew on briefs jerkily, and grabbed for the shirt and suit he had never seen before. He was no longer thinking, now. Blind panic was winning. He thrust his feet into shoes, not bothering with socks.

A slip of paper fell from his coat, with big sprawled Greek letters. He saw only the last line as it fell to the floor—some equation that ended with an infinity sign. Then psi and alpha, connected by a dash. The alpha sign had been scratched out, and something written over it. He tried to reach it, and more papers spilled from his coat pocket. The fear washed up more strongly. He forgot the papers. Even the cigarettes were too far away for him to return to them. His wallet lay on the chair, and he barely grabbed it before the urge overpowered him completely.

The doorknob slipped in his sweating hands, but he managed to turn it. The elevator wasn't at his floor, and he couldn't stop for it. His feet pounded on the stairs, taking him down the three floors to the street at a breakneck pace. The walls of the stairway seemed to be rushing together, as if trying to close the way. He screamed at them, until they were behind, and he was charging out of the front door.

A half-drunken couple was coming in—a fat, older man and a slim girl he barely saw. He hit them, throwing them aside. He jerked from the entrance. Cars were streaming down West End Avenue. He dashed across, paying no attention to them. His rush carried him onto the opposite sidewalk. Then, finally, the blind panic left him, and he was leaning against a building, gasping for breath, and wondering whether his heart could endure the next beat.

Across the street, the fat man he had hit was coming after him. Hawkes gathered himself together to apologize, but the words never came. A second blinding horror hit at him, and his eyes darted up towards the windows of his apartment.

PURSUIT

It was only a tiny glow, at first, like a drop from the heart of a sun. Then, before he could more than blink, it spread, until the whole apartment seemed to blaze. A gout of smoke poured from the shattering window, and a dull concussion struck his ears.

The infernally bright flame flickered, leaped outward from the window, and died down almost as quickly as it had come, leaving twisted, half-molten metal where the window frames had been.

They'd almost gotten him! Hawkes felt his legs weaken and quiver, while his eyes remained glued to the spot that had lighted the whole street a second before. They'd tried—but he'd escaped in time.

It must have been a thermite bomb—nothing but thermite could be that hot. He had never imagined that even such a bomb could give so much heat so quickly. Where? In the tape-recorder?

He waited numbly, expecting more fire, but the brief flame seemed to have died out completely. He shook his head, unbelieving, and started to cross the street again, to survey the damage or to join the crowd that was beginning to collect.

*

The fear surged up in him again, halting his step as if he'd struck a physical barrier. With it came the sound of an auto-horn, the button held down permanently. His eyes darted down the street, to see a long, gray sedan with old-fashioned running-boards come around the corner on two wheels. Its brakes screeched, and it skidded to a halt beside Hawkes' apartment building.

A slim young man in gray tweeds leaped out of it and came to a stop. He threw back heavy black hair with a toss of his head and ran into the crowd that parted to let him through. Someone began pointing towards Hawkes.

Hawkes tried to slide around the corner without being seen, but a flashlight in the young man's hands pinpointed him. A yell went up.

"There he goes!"

His feet sounded hopelessly on the sidewalk as he dashed up toward Broadway, but behind came the sound of others in pursuit, and the shouting was becoming a meaningless babble as others took it up. There was no longer any doubt. Someone was certainly after him—there'd been no time to turn in an alarm over the fire in his apartment. They'd been coming for him before that started.

What hideous crime could he have committed during the period he couldn't remember? Or what spy-ring had encircled him?

He had no time to think of the questions, even. He ducked into the thin swarm of a few people leaving a theater just as the pursuing group rounded the corner, with the slim young man in the lead.

Their cries were enough. Hands reached for him from the theater crowd, and a foot stretched out to trip him up. Terror lent speed to his legs, but he could never outdistance them, as long as others picked up the chase.

A sudden blast of heat struck down, and the air was golden and hazy above him. He staggered sideways, blinded by the glare. The crowd was screaming in fear now, no longer holding him back. He felt the edge of a subway entrance. There was no other choice. He ducked down the steps, while his vision slowly returned, and risked a glance back at the street—just as the whole entrance came down in a wreck of broken wood and metal.

A clap of thundering noise sounded above him, drowning the hoarse screams of the people. The few persons in the station rushed for the fallen entrance, to mill about it crazily, just as a train pulled in. Hawkes started toward it, and then realized his pursuers would suspect that. Whatever frightful weapon had been used against him had back-fired on them—but they'd catch him at the next stop.

*

He found space at the end of the platform and dropped off, skirting behind the train, and avoiding the the high-voltage rails.

The uptown platform held only three people, and they seemed to be too busy at the other end, trying to see the wreckage, to notice him. He vaulted onto it, and dashed into the men's room. The few contents of his coat pocket came out quickly, and he began to stuff

PURSUIT

them into his trousers. He shoved the coat into a garbage can, wet his hair and slicked it back, and opened his shirt collar. The change didn't make much of a disguise, but they wouldn't be expecting him to show up so near where he entered.

His skin prickled as he came out, but he fought down the sickness in his stomach. A few drops of rain were beginning to fall, and the crowd around the accident was thinning out. That might help him—or it might prove more dangerous. He had to chance it.

He stopped to buy a paper, maintaining an air of casual interest in the crowd.

"What happened?" he asked.

The newsstand attendant jerked his eyes back from they excitement reluctantly. "Damned if I know. Someone, says a ball lightning came down and broke over there. Caved in the entrance. Nobody's hurt seriously, they say. I was just stacking up to go home when I heard it go off. Didn't see it. Just saw the entrance falling in."

Hawkes picked up his change and turned back across Broadway, pretending he was studying the paper. The dateline showed it was July 10, just seven months from the beginning of his memory lapse. He couldn't believe that there had been time enough for any group to invent a heat-ray, if such a thing could exist. Yet nothing else would explain the two sudden bursts of flame he had seen. Even if it could be invented, it would hardly be used in public for anything less than a National Emergency.

What had happened in the seven blanked-out months?

II

The room was smelly and cheap, with dirty walls and no carpet on the floor, but it was a relief after the hours of tramping and riding about the city. Hawkes sat on the rickety chair, letting the wetness dry out of his clothes. He looked at the bed, trying to convince himself he could strip and warm up there while his clothes dried. But something in his head warned him that he couldn't—he'd have to be ready to run again. The same urge had made him demand a room on the ground floor, where he could escape through the window if they found him. They could never find him here—but they would! Sooner or later, whatever was after him would come!

It had seemed simple enough, before. There had been three friends he could trust. Seven months, he had felt, couldn't have killed their faith in him, no matter what he'd done. And perhaps he'd been right, though there'd been no chance to test it.

He'd almost been caught at the first place. The two men outside had seemed to be no more than a couple of friends awaiting for a bus. Only the approach of another man who resembled Hawkes had tipped him off, by the quick interest they had shown.

The other places had also been posted—and beyond the third, he'd seen the gray sedan with the running boards, parked back in the shadows, waiting.

There had been less than ten dollars in his wallet, and most of that had gone for cab fares. He'd barely had enough left for this dingy room, the later edition of the newspaper, and the coffee and donuts that lay beside him, half-consumed.

He glanced toward the door, listening with quick fear as steps sounded on the stairs. Then he drew his breath in again, and reached for the newspaper. But it told him as little as the first one had.

This one mentioned the two mysterious explosions of "ball lightning" in a feature on the first page, but only as curiosities. They even gave his address and listed the apartment as being in his name, though apparently not currently occupied. But no other reference was made to him, or to the chase.

He shook his head at that. He couldn't see a newspaper-man refusing to make a story of it, if there was any other news about him to which they could tie the burning of his apartment. Apparently it was not the police who were after him, and he hadn't been guilty of anything so ordinary as murder.

*

PURSUIT

Outside the window, a sudden scream sounded, and he jerked from the chair, reaching the door before he realized it was only a cat on the prowl. He shuddered, his old hatred of cats coming to the surface. For a minute, he thought of shutting the window. But he couldn't cut off his chance to retreat through the garbage-littered back-yard.

He returned to his search, beginning an inventory of the few belongings that had been in his pocket. There was a notebook, and he scanned it rapidly. A few pages were missing, and most were blank. There was only a shopping list. That puzzled him for a minute—he couldn't believe he'd taken to using lipstick as well as cigarettes, though both were listed in his handwriting. The notebook contained nothing else.

He stuffed it back into his pockets, along with his keyring. There were more keys than he'd expected, some of which were strange to him, but none held any mark that would identify them. He put a few pennies into another pocket—his entire wealth, now, in a world where no more money would be available to him. He grimaced, dropping a comb into the same pocket.

Then there was only his wallet left. His identification card was there, unchanged. Behind it, where his wife's picture had always been, there was only a folded clipping. He drew it out, hoping for a clew. It was only an announcement of people killed in an airplane crash—and among those found dead was Mrs. Wilbur Hawkes, of New York. It seemed that Irma had never reached Reno for the divorce.

He tried to feel some sorrow at that, but time must have healed whatever hurt there had been, even though he couldn't remember. She had hated him ever since she'd found that he really wasn't willing to please his father by becoming another of the vice-presidents in the old man's bank, with an unearned but fancy salary. He'd preferred teaching mathematics and dabbling with a bit of research into the probable value of the ESP work being done at Duke University. He'd explained why he hated banking; Irma had made it clear that she really needed the mink coat no assistant professor could afford. It had been stalemate—a bitter, seven-year stalemate, until she finally gave up hope and demanded a divorce.

He threw the clipping away, and pulled out the final bit of paper. It was a rent receipt for a cold-water apartment on the poorer section of West End—from the price of eighteen dollars a month, it had to be a cold-water place. He frowned, considering it. Apartment 12. That might explain why his own apartment had been unused, though it made little sense to him. It would probably be watched by now, anyway.

*

He jerked to his feet at a sound on the window-sill, but it was only a cat, eyeing the unfinished donut. He threw the food out, and the cat dived after it. Hawkes waited for the touch of ice along his backbone to go away. It didn't.

This time, he tried to ignore it. He picked up the paper and began going through it, looking for something that might give him some slight clew. But there was nothing there. Only a heading on an inside page that stirred his curiosity.

Scientist Seeks Confinement

He glanced at it, noting that a Professor Meinzer, formerly of City College, had appeared at Bellevue, asking to be put away in a padded cell, preferably with a strait-jacket. The Professor had only explained that he considered himself dangerous to society. No other reason was found. Professor Meinzer had been doing private work, believed to relate to his theory that....

The panic was back, thick in Hawkes' throat. He jerked back against the wall, his heart racing, while he tried to fight it down. There was no sound from the hall or outside. He forced his eyes back to the paper.

And the paper was surrounded by a golden haze. It burst into a momentary flame as the haze flickered out. Hawkes dropped the ashes from his clammy hands. He hadn't been burned!

PURSUIT

You can't escape. Run. They'll get you!

He heard the outside door open, as it had opened a hundred times. But now it could only mean that more were coming. He jerked for the open window.

Something came sailing through the air to hit the sill. Hawkes screamed weakly, far down in his throat, before his eyes could register the fact that it was only the cat again.

Then the cat let out a horrible beginning of a sound, and its poor, half-starved body seemed to turn inside out, with a churning motion that Hawkes could barely see. Blood and gore spattered from it, striking his face and clothes.

He froze, unable to move. Either they were outside in the yard, or whatever frightful weapon they used could work through a closed door. He tried to move, first one way, then the other. His feet remained frozen.

Then steps sounded in the hallway, and he waited no longer. His legs came to sudden life, hurling him over the carcass of the cat and outside. He went charging through the refuse, and then leaped and clawed his way over the fence. The alley was deserted, and he shot down it, to swing right, and into another alley.

It wasn't until his muscles began to fail that he could control himself enough to stop and stumble into a darkened spot among the garbage cans, spent and gasping for breath.

*

There was no sign of anyone following. Hawkes had no idea of how they could trace him—but he was beginning to suspect that nothing was impossible, judging by the results of their weapons. For the moment, though, he seemed to have shaken off pursuit. And the physical fatigue had apparently eased some of his terror.

What had shocked him into losing seven months out of his memory, and still could drive him into absolute terror at the first sign of them?

LESTER DEL REY

He couldn't go back to the room, and his own apartment was out of the question. The rain had stopped, mercifully, but he couldn't walk the streets indefinitely, dirty and bedraggled as he was. He tried to think of something to do, but all of his schemes took money which he no longer had.

Finally, he arose wearily. Maybe the apartment for which he had the rent receipt was watched—but he'd have to chance it. There was no place else.

He'd been accidentally heading toward it, and he continued now, sticking to the alleys until he reached West End Avenue. He tried to hurry, but the best his tired muscles could do was a slow shuffle.

Light was beginning to show faintly in the sky, but it was still too early for more than a few cars and a chance pedestrian. At this hour, the avenue was used by only a few cruising cabs, heading toward better sections. He shuffled along, trying to look like a man on his way home after too much night out. The cat blood on his clothes bothered him, until he tried weaving a little as he walked, imitating the drunks he had seen often enough.

He passed an all night diner, and fished for his pennies. But there were several men inside. He went on, past Fifty-ninth Street, heading for the apartment, which should be near Sixty-seventh.

He was just reaching the top of the hill near Sixty-fourth when a gray sedan sped along, heading downtown. There were running boards on it, and behind the wheel sat the slim young man who'd given chase to Hawkes before.

Hawkes tried to duck, but the sedan was already braking and swinging back. It was beside him before he could realize more than the old clamor of his brain, telling him to run, that he couldn't escape.

The car matched his speed, and the driver leaned far to the right. "Will Hawkes," the young man called. "How about a lift?"

PURSUIT

The smile was pleasant, and the voice was casual, as if they were old friends. There was no gun in the man's hands. It might have been any honest offer of a ride.

Hawkes braced himself, just as a patrol car turned onto the Avenue ahead. He opened his mouth to scream, but his vocal cords were frozen. The young man followed his eyes to the patrol car, and frowned.

Then the gray sedan lifted smoothly upwards to a height of twenty feet, turned sharply in mid-air, lifted again, and seemed to make a smooth landing on top of a huge garage building!

There had been no roar of jets and no evidence of any means of propulsion.

*

The patrol car went on down the Avenue, heading for the diner. The officers inside apparently had missed the whole affair.

Hawkes' cowardly legs suddenly came unfrozen. He was conscious of them churning madly. With an effort, he got partial control of himself, managing to focus on the house numbers.

There were no watchers outside the number he wanted, though they could have been in rooms across the street. He had no choice, now. He leaped up the steps and into the hallway. His eyes darted around, spotting a door that led out to the side, probably into an alley. He drew himself together, hiding behind the stairs.

But there was no further pursuit for the moment. The fear that seemed to come before each attack was missing. Maybe it meant he was safe for the moment—though it hadn't warned him of the car the young man was driving.

Heat rays! Levitation! Hawkes dropped to his knees as fatigue and reaction caught up with him again, but his mind churned over the new evidence. As a mathematician, he was sure such things could not exist. If they did, there would have been extension of math well in advance of the perfection of the machines, and he'd have known of it as speculative theory, at least. Yet, without such evidence, the devices apparently existed.

The police weren't in on it, that much was certain. It was more than a hunt for a criminal. What had been going on during the months he had missed?

His mind shuttled over the spy-thrillers he had seen. If some nation had the secrets, and he had discovered them.... But the heat ray would never have been used openly, then; they wouldn't tip their hand. Anyhow, the cold war was still going on, and that would have been pointless when any nation had such power.

And if the secret belonged to the United States, the young man would never have levitated to avoid police at the greater risk of tipping off anyone who saw that such things could be done.

Nothing made sense—not even the crazy feeling of fear that had warned him on some occasions and failed him this last time. The only explanation that was credible was the totally incredible idea that some life, alien to earth and with strange unearthly powers, was after him—or that he was insane.

He fumbled through a pack of cigarettes until he located the last one, streaked with sweat that was still pouring down from his armpit, and lighted it. It was all answer-less—just as his sudden need for smoking was.

III

Hawkes crushed out the cigarette and began climbing the wide stairs slowly. It was probably an ambush into which he was heading—but without this place, he had no chance of resting. He stared at the numbers painted on the dirty red doors, and went on up a second flight of stairs. The number he wanted was at the end of the hall, dimly lighted. He dropped to the keyhole, but found it had been filled long ago, probably when the Yale lock was installed.

He put his ear against the door and listened. There was no sound from inside except a monotonous noise that must be water dripping

PURSUIT

from a leaky faucet. Finally, he climbed to his feet and reached for his keys. The third one he tried fitted, and the door swung open.

He fumbled about, looking for a light switch, and finally struck a match. The switch was a string hanging down from a bare bulb. He pulled it, to find he stood inside one of the old monstrosities with which New York is filled—a combination kitchen and bathroom, with a tiny closet for the toilet in one corner. There was an ice-box, a dirty stove, a Franklin heater connected to the chimney, a small sink, and a rickety table with four folding chairs. In a closet, cheap china showed.

He went through that, into the seven-by-twelve living room. There was a cheap radio, a worn sofa, two more folding chairs and a big typing table. The rug on the floor had been patched together. Then he breathed more easily. Over the back of one of the chairs was a sports jacket which he recognized as his own. He jerked it up suddenly and began going through the pockets, but they had already been emptied.

It didn't matter—he no longer cared why he should be in a place so totally unlike any his usually neat habits would have led him to. It was his.

Then, as he came into the bedroom, he hesitated. It was smaller than the living room, with a bed that took up half of one wall, and two dressers jammed into the remaining space. One corner held a cardboard closet—and hanging on the hook was a man's raincoat and hat, both at least five sizes too big for him. His eyes darted about, to find a strange mixture of things he remembered as his and possessions which he would never have owned. On one of the dressers was a small traveling case, filled with the cosmetics and appliances which only a woman would use.

He jerked open the closet, and his nose told him before his eyes that it held only female clothing! Yet on the shelf his old hat rested happily.

LESTER DEL REY

He could make no sense of it—the place looked as if several people lived in it, and yet it wasn't really fitted for anyone to spend his whole time there. There was none of the accumulation of property that would fit any permanent residence. He went out of the bedroom, passing the typewriter desk. The typewriter was an old, standard Olympia—a German machine he'd refitted with the Dvorak keyboard which he had learned for greater efficiency. He was sure nobody else would want it.

The dishes were dusty, and there was no food in the ice-box.

*

Now, though, it began to fit—a place where it was convenient to stop in, but not a place to live. And perhaps he had been in the habit of lending it to others. Though why he shouldn't have used his own apartment was something he still couldn't understand.

But it was possible there was no record of this place.

He began shucking off his shirt as he went back through the living room—until the marks on the rug caught his eyes. Something heavy had rested there recently—there had been other desks about, or heavily laden tables. And a bit of paper under the sofa could only have come from one of the complicated computing machines used in high-power mathematics. He scanned the fragment, making no sense of it, except that it was esoteric enough to belong to any new branch of theory. For a second, the heat-rays and levitations entered his head—but none of the symbols fitted such a branch of physical development.

What had been going on here—and why had the machines been removed so recently that their traces still looked fresh?

He shook his head—and froze, as a key turned in the lock.

There was no time for flight. She stood in the doorway, blinking at the light before he could turn. She, of course, was the girl whom he'd barely noticed when he knocked the couple down as he charged out of his apartment.

PURSUIT

Of course? He puzzled over that. He'd almost expected it—and yet, now that he looked more closely, he couldn't even be sure that she was the same. She wore the same green jacket, but nothing else he could be sure of, because he had no other memory of that girl. This one was two inches shorter than he was, with dark red hair and the deepest blue eyes he had seen. She looked like an artist's conception of an Irish colleen, except that her mouth was open half an inch, and she was studying him with the look of being about ready to scream.

"Who are you?" He forced the words out at her.

She shook her head, and then smiled doubtfully. "Ellen Ibañez, naturally. You startled me! But you must be Wilbur Hawkes, of course. Didn't you get my wire?"

He watched her, but there had been no stumbling over his name, and no effort to make it sound too casual. Apparently, the name meant nothing to her. He shook his head. "What wire?" Then he plunged ahead, quickly. "You've heard of amnesia? Good. Well, I've got it—partially. If you can tell me anything about myself before yesterday, Miss, I'll never be anything but...."

He choked on that, unable to finish. And behind the surface emotions, his mind was poised, sniffing for danger. There was no feeling of it, though he kept telling himself alternately that she had been the girl at the door and that she obviously had not been.

He'd seen her before. The tilt of her head, that unmatchable hair....

*

"You poor man!" Her voice was all sympathy, and the bag she was carrying dropped to the floor as she came over. "You mean you *really* can't remember—at all?"

"Not for the last seven months!"

She seemed surprised. "But that was when you answered my advertisement. I never saw you—though you did call me, and your voice sounds familiar. You sent me the check, and I mailed you the key. That was all."

LESTER DEL REY

"But I must have given you references—told you something—"

Again, she shook her head. "Nothing. You said you were a teacher at CCNY, but that you were quitting, and wanted a place to use as an office. You didn't care what it was like. That's all."

Hawkes felt she was lying—but it could have been true. And in his present state, he probably believed everyone was other than they seemed. He remembered the gray sedan rising to the roof—and the cat turning inside out—

Sickness hit at him. He groped back towards a chair, sinking into it. He'd almost found a refuge, and even hoped that he could find some of the missing past. Now....

He must have partially fainted. He heard vague sounds, and then she was putting something against his lips. It was bitter and hot, though it only remotely resembled coffee. He gulped it gratefully, not caring that it was sweet and black. He saw the bottle of old coffee powder, caked with age, and heard the water boiling on the stove. Idly, he wondered whether he'd bought the jar originally or she had. Then his senses snapped back.

"Thanks," he muttered thickly. He groped his way to his feet, his head slowly clearing. "I guess I'd better go now."

She forced him back into the chair. "You're in no condition to leave here, Will Hawkes. Ugh! Your shoes are filthy. Let me help you ... there, isn't that better? Whatever you've been doing to yourself, you should be ashamed. You're going straight to bed while I clean some of this up!"

His head had sunk back on the table, and everything reached him through a thick fog. It wasn't right—girls didn't act that way to strange men who looked as if they'd come from a Bowery fight. Girls didn't take a man's clothes off. Girls didn't....

He let her half carry him into the bedroom, and tried to protest as she put him between clean sheets. He stared at the view of his lavender shorts against the fresh whiteness, while things seemed far away. He'd played with a girl named Ellen, once when he was eleven

PURSUIT

and she was nine. She'd had bright copper hair, and her name had been—what had it been? Not Ibañez. Bennett, that was it. Ellen Bennett.

He must have said it aloud. She chuckled. "Of course, Will. Though I never thought you'd be the same Will Hawkes. I knew it when I saw that scar on your shoulder, where you cut yourself sliding down our cellar door. Go to sleep."

Sliding down, sliding down into clouds of sleep. Sleep! She'd drugged him! Something in the coffee!

*

He jerked up, reaching for her, but she ducked aside, drawing on the tops to a pair of frilly pajamas. "Ellen, you—"

"Shh!" She pulled a robe over the pajamas and lay down, outside the blankets. "Shh, Will. You have to sleep. You're *so* tired, *so* sleepy...."

Her voice was soothing, and the fingers along the base of his neck was relaxing. He reached out a last inquiring finger of doubt for the feeling of danger, and couldn't find it. This was as wrong as the other things had been wrong—but his mind let go, and he was suddenly asleep.

He awoke slowly, with a thick feeling in his mouth. Drugged! And the sense of danger had failed him again! He swung over sharply, reaching for her, but she was gone.

His clothes lay beside him, neatly pressed, and he grabbed for them. There was a pair of socks, too large, but better than none. His muscles felt wrong as he began dressing, but the feeling wore away. The clock said that less than two hours had passed. If she'd put a drug in the coffee, it must have been one to which he was less sensitive than the average. She'd probably never suspected that he would waken.

A trace of fear struck through him, but it was weaker than before, and it seemed normal enough, under the circumstances. He fumbled over the shoelaces, and then grabbed up his coat.

LESTER DEL REY

She'd bring *them* back! Maybe they'd used her as a spy!

But he couldn't understand why she'd bothered to press his clothes. And the apartment still puzzled him. Even if her story was true, it simply wasn't the sort of a place where a girl like her would live. Nor was it fixed as she might have arranged a place, even allowing for what he might have done to it in seven months.

He reached automatically for the lock in the dim hall, and realized his hands knew the door, whatever else was true. Then he went out and down the stairs. He heard a babble of kids' voices, part in English and part in a sort of Spanish. That meant that things were normal, to the casual observer along the street. But he knew it was poor evidence that things really were as they should be. He stood in the comparative darkness of the hall, staring out. Nothing was wrong, so far as he could see. He had to risk it.

Hawkes shoved past the women on the steps and headed down West End, trying not to seem in a hurry. His eyes turned up to the roof of the garage, but he could see nothing there; he'd half-expected that the slim young man would be parked up on the roof, waiting.

*

Then the fear began, mounting slowly. He jerked around quickly, scanning the street. For a second, he thought he saw the slim figure, but it was only a back turned to him, and it disappeared into a barber-shop. Probably someone else.

The fear mounted a little, and he found his steps quickening. He cut around the corner, where men were crowded into a little restaurant. He was heading into a dead-end street, but there was an alley leading from it. He had to keep off the main streets.

Footsteps sounded behind him.

He moved faster, and the footsteps also speeded up. He slowed, and they kept on. Then they were nearly behind him, just as he reached the alley and jerked back into it, grabbing for a broken bottle he had spotted.

PURSUIT

"Will!" It was a gasping wheeze. "Will! For God's sake, it's only me. I know everything—your amnesia. But let me explain!"

It stopped him. He held the bottle carefully, as the fat figure of an old man stepped softly around the corner, fear written on every aged wrinkle. It was the man he'd stumbled into when he dashed out of his apartment.

But the fear there matched his own so completely that he dropped the bottle. The other man stood trembling, gasping for breath. Then he gathered himself together, though his pudgy hands still clenched tightly, showing white knuckles.

"Will," he repeated. "You must believe me. I know about you. I want to help you—if there's any help for you, God forgive us both. And God have mercy on Earth. It's worse than you can believe—and different. It's...."

Horror washed over the old man's face. He stood, fighting within himself. Hawkes felt his own back hairs lift, and he drew back. For a second, the fat man seemed to waver before him, as if his body was only a projection. Then it quieted.

"It—it almost had me for a second."

He turned back to Hawkes, trying to control the quivering muscles in his face. But his victory was still incomplete when he suddenly leaped up.

"Get back, Will. Oh, God, O God!"

He leaped outwards, his fat old legs pumping savagely. Then the air seemed to quiver.

Where he had been, there was only a dark cloud of smoke, spreading outwards in a rough equivalent of his shape. A spurt of steam leaped upwards savagely, and the smoke seemed darker. It began to drift on the air, touched a building, and left a spot of smudginess, before it drifted on, getting thinner with each gust of wind. It was as if every atom of his body had suddenly disassociated itself from every other atom.

*

LESTER DEL REY

Hawkes found his fingernails cutting his palms, and there was blood flowing from his bitten tongue. He heard a hacking moan in his throat. He struggled against something that seemed to be holding him down, and then leaped at least ten feet, to land running.

The alley was twisted and narrow. He shot down it and around a corner. An ice-house stood there, and he barely avoided the loading trucks. He was back near the apartment building where he'd found the girl, and he doubled to a door that showed. It seemed to be locked, but somehow, he got through it. He seemed to melt through the door, though he wasn't sure whether his lunge smashed it or whether his fingers had found the latch in time.

He ducked around loose-hanging electric wires, under twisted pipes, and across a pile of coal around a hot-water heater. He twisted and turned, to come into complete darkness, and halt short, listening.

The fear was going—and there were again no sounds of pursuit. But he couldn't be sure. He'd heard no sounds when the fat man had leaped out, but they had been there.

Silently and thickly, he cursed. To find a man who seemed to be his friend, and who knew about him—and then to have them kill that man with such horrible efficiency before he could learn what it was all about!

He gagged in the darkness, almost fainting again.

Then, slowly, it was too much. For the moment, he could run no more, and nothing seemed to matter. He understood his sudden bravado no better than the unnatural cowardice that had been riding his shoulders, but he shrugged, and moved forward.

The dark passage led out to steps, that carried him up to the sidewalk, in front of the building. Ellen Ibañez—or Bennett—was less than five feet from him, and her eyes were fixed firmly on his face.

PURSUIT IV

LESTER DEL REY

She seemed surprised, but tried to smile. "I thought I left you asleep, Will," she said, in a tone that was meant to be bantering. "'Smatter, the fuse blow?"

He accepted the excuse for his presence in the basement. "Yeah, it did. You left the iron on. I wondered what happened to you?"

"Nothing. Just shopping. There wasn't a bit of food in the place—and I must say, Will, you aren't much of a housekeeper. I bought pounds of soap!"

He followed her up the stairs, and his key opened the door. He was still operating on the general belief that they'd be least likely to spot him where they had already found him once. If the girl had tipped them off, then they had it figured out that he had run off, and probably wouldn't be back.

He hoped so, at any rate.

She was talking too briskly, and she was too careful not to mention that the iron was cool, with its cord wrapped neatly around the handle. He offered no explanation, but let her babble on about the strange coincidence of his being *the* Will Hawkes, and how she'd almost forgotten the childhood days.

"How come the Ibañez?" he asked, finally.

"Stage name! I tried to make a go of the musicals, but it wasn't my line, I found. But the name stuck."

"And where'd you learn how to drug coffee that way?"

She didn't change expression. There was even a touch of a twinkle in her eye. "Waitress in a combination bar and restaurant. You needed the sleep, Will. And I guess I still feel as much of a mother to you as I did when you used to get hurt, so long ago."

She had things out of the bags now, and he saw that she had been doing a lot of shopping. There had still been time enough to call the slim young man, though—or, he suddenly realized, the fat man. He had no more reason to believe her an enemy than a friend. Then he corrected that. If she'd known enough to call the fat man, and had

PURSUIT

been his friend, she could have told him things. She'd denied knowing anything, though.

He couldn't understand why he trusted her—and yet, somehow, he did. Even if he knew she'd called them, he would still have to trust her. He was sure now that she was lying, and that she had been the girl at the door—but that meant she'd been with the fat man. And the fat man had seemed to be his friend. Or, had the man been set to lure him out, but miscalculated, and gotten only what had been meant for him?

His head was spinning, and he gave it up. He was a fool to trust her simply because the fear feeling subsided around her—but he had nothing better to do than to follow his hunches, and then try to play the odds as best he could.

*

"Cigarettes," she said, handing him a pack of his brand. "And for me. Shoe dye—your shoes need it, and I couldn't find a shoe store. I did get a shirt though, and a tie. You'll find a hat in that bag. Size seven and a quarter?"

He nodded gratefully, and went in to change. His old shirt had caught most of the cat's blood, and he needed a fresh one. There were a couple of spots on his trousers, but they'd do. And the sports jacket matched well enough. He daubed the dye onto his shoes—one of the combined polish and dye things.

"Cold-cuts all right?" she asked, and he called back a vague answer that seemed to satisfy her. He was staring at the shoe dye.

It worked fairly well, when he experimented. He daubed it onto his hair with a wisp of cotton. His hair began to mat down, but he found that combing it out as he went along removed the worst of the wax and still left some of the color. It worked better than it should have done.

He found a bottle of something that smelled of alcohol and belonged in her cosmetics, and began removing most of the mess. By being careful, he got the wax and most of the dye smell off, while leaving his hair darker.

"Better wash up," she called.

There was a razor among the things she had bought. He daubed some of the dye on his upper lip, where the stubble of a mustache was showing. It was easier there, if it didn't wash off in soap and water.

Some of it did, but when he finished shaving, he felt better. It wouldn't pass close inspection, but he now seemed to have darker hair, and the dye had exaggerated the little beginning of a mustache enough to make some change in his appearance.

He waited for her to comment, but she said nothing. He waited for her questions about what he was going to do, and her explanations that of course he couldn't stay there. She merely went on talking idly, while they ate. It didn't fit.

Finally he stood up and began taking down the rope that was strung up over one end of the room, to use as a clothes line, he supposed. She looked up at that. "What—"

"You can fight, if you want to," he told her. "Or you can save yourself the headache of being knocked out. Take your choice. People don't pay much attention to screams in a place like this. And I'm not going to harm you, if you'll take it easily."

"You mean it!" Her eyes were huge in her face, and there was a touch of fright now. She gulped visibly, and then seemed to go limp. "All right, Will. In the bedroom?"

He nodded, and she went ahead of him. She didn't struggle, until he was about to gag her. Then she drew her head aside. "There's money in my bag, if you're going out."

*

He swore, hotly and sickly. If she'd only act just once as a normal female should! Maybe Irma had been a hysterical, cold-blooded fool, but she couldn't have been that much different from other women—even the books indicated Ellen should be anything but so damned coöperative!

PURSUIT

"If you'll tell me what's going on, I'll still let you go," he suggested, drawing her hands tighter together.

"I can't, Will. I don't know."

He had to believe her—he knew she was telling the truth, at least to some extent. And that made it just so much worse. He bound the gag over her mouth as gently as he could, and closed the door behind him. Her big eyes haunted him as he turned to the telephone.

The information girl at CCNY could only tell him that Wilbur Hawkes had resigned abruptly seven months before, and no one knew where he was—they had heard he was doing government research. He snorted at that—it was always the excuse, when nobody knew anything.

He tried a few other numbers, and gave up. Nobody knew—and nobody seemed to react to his name any differently from what they would have done had he remained a quiet, professorish man, minding his own business, instead of being chased by....

He couldn't complete that. The idea was still too fantastic. Even if there were alien life-forms that were subtly invading Earth, why should they pick on him? What good could a little, unimportant mathematician do them—particularly if they had the powers he already knew they possessed? It was a poor answer, though no harder to believe than that any group on Earth could so suddenly come up with miracles.

Anyhow, men knew enough already to be pretty sure that Mars and Venus wouldn't have creatures that could invade Earth—and the other planets were hopeless. Perhaps from another star—but that would mean violating the theories of mass-increase with the speed of light, and he was not ready to accept that, yet.

This time, he went out of the building without looking first. It could do no good—they could hide from him, he knew, and he would only call attention to himself by looking around. With the change in appearance, he might get by. He moved rapidly up to Broadway, where he found a little clothing store and a ready-made suit that

LESTER DEL REY

nearly fitted him. The tailor there seemed unconcerned when he insisted the cuffs be turned up at once, and that he wanted to wear it immediately. It took nearly an hour, but he felt safe, for a change. A five-and-ten furnished a pair of heavy-rimmed glasses that seemed to have blanks in them, and he decided he might get by.

There was no evidence of pursuit. He caught a cab, and headed for the library. Ellen had been well-heeled—suspiciously so for a girl who lived in a cold-water flat like that; he'd peeled fifteen tens from her wallet, and there'd been more, not to mention the twenties. His conscience bothered him a bit, but he was in no position to worry too much.

*

The library was still the puzzle of the ages to him—he'd used it half his life, and still found it impossible to guess why such a building had been chosen. But eventually, he found the periodical room, and managed to get through the red tape enough to be given a small table with a stack of newspapers and magazines.

The mathematics magazines interested him most. He pored through them, looking for a single hint of the things he had seen. Einstein's work with gravity stood out, but no real advances had come from it. It was still a philosophical rather than an actual attack on physics—as beautiful as a new theology, and about as hard to utilize. He skimmed, through the pages, but nothing showed. No real advance had been made since his memory blanked out, except for one paper on variable stars which was interesting, but unhelpful.

He threw them aside in disgust. He knew that it was useless to look in other languages. Work couldn't be done without some first stages that would be reported, and any significant new theory would be picked up and spread. Science wasn't yet completely under political wraps.

For a second, he stopped as he came to a paper bearing his by-line. Then he grimaced—it was an old one, just published—his attempt to find how the phenomena of poltergeists could be fitted into the

PURSUIT

conservation of energy, and his final proof that the whole business was sheer rubbish. It would be nice to be able to get back to a life where he could fool around with such learned jokes.

The newspapers, beginning with the last day he could remember, were almost as barren of results. There was the story of the cold war, without the strange overtones that should be there if any of the major powers—where all the major scientists would tend to be—had found something new. He'd studied the statistical analysis of mob psychology at times, and felt sure he could spot the signs.

He skimmed on, without results, until he finally came to the current paper. This he read more carefully. There was no mention of him. But he found something on the fat man. It was a simple followup to the story about the scientist who'd turned himself in at Bellevue—the man had mysteriously disappeared, three hours later. And there was a picture—the face of the fat man, with "Professor Arthur Meinzer" under it.

It didn't help.

Hawkes shoved the magazines and papers back, and went through the series of halls and stairs that led him to the main reference room, inconveniently located on the top floor. He found the book he wanted, and thumbed rapidly through it. Meinzer was listed on the bottom of page 972—but as he looked for 973, a pile of ashes dribbled onto the floor.

There was no use. They'd gotten there ahead of him.

He made one final attempt. He called the college, asking for Meinzer, to find that nobody even knew the name! He knew they were lying—but he could do nothing about that. Maybe it was only because of the publicity—or maybe because someone or something had gotten to them first!

*

Fear was growing with him as he came out on the street. He ducked into a crowd, and headed slowly into a corner drug store, trying to

LESTER DEL REY

seem inconspicuous, but the fear mounted. They were near—they would get him! Run, GO!

He fought it down, and found that it was weakened, either by his becoming used to it or because the urgency was less than it had been.

He ducked into a phone-booth and called the newspaper, keeping his eye on both entrances to the store. It seemed to take forever to locate the proper man there, but finally he had his connection.

"Meinzer," the voice said, with a curious doubtfulness.

"Oh, yeah. Mister, that story's dead! Call up...."

The telephone melted slowly, dropping into a little cold puddle on the floor!

Hawkes had felt the tension mounting, and he was prepared for anything. Now he found himself on the street, darting across Forty-second Street against the light, without even remembering having left the booth. He stole a quick glance back, to see people staring at him with open mouths. He thought he saw a slim figure in gray tweeds, but he couldn't be sure—and there were probably thousands of such men in New York.

He ducked into a bank, wormed his way around the various aisles, and out the back entrance. A cab was waiting there, and he held out a bill.

"I'm late, buddy. Penn Station!"

The cab-driver took the bill and the hint, and darted out, just as the light was changing.

Penn Station was as good a place to try to get lost from pursuit as any. Hawkes examined his wallet, considering trying to get a train out—but he'd used up nearly all he had taken from Ellen.

And all his careful disguise had proved useless. They weren't fooled—and this business of dodging was wearing thin. By now, they'd know his habits!

He drew out a coin, flipping it. It came up heads. He frowned, but there was nothing else to do. He moved down the ramp toward the subway that would carry him back to Sixty-sixth and Broadway. He

PURSUIT

was probably walking into their trap by now, but the coin was right. He had to free Ellen. If they got him, it couldn't be much worse for him.

Then he shuddered. He couldn't know whether it would be worse for his country, or even his world. He couldn't really know anything.

V

It was growing dark as he walked down Sixty-sixth, eyeing every man suspiciously, and knowing his suspicion would do no good. He was still trying to think, though he knew his thoughts were as useless as his suspicions.

If he could remember! His mind came up sharply against leaving Irma and taking out the mail; then it went abruptly blank. What had been in the letter? It had been from a professor—it might have been from Professor Meinzer. That would tie in neatly. But Meinzer was dead, and he couldn't remember. They'd stripped him of his memory. How? Why? Were they trying to prevent his giving information to others—or were they trying to get something from him? And what could he know?

He'd dabbled with ESP mathematically, but now he found himself wondering if it could exist. Could they be tracking him by some natural or mechanical ability to read his mind? He strained his own mind to find a whisper of foreign thought, outside his brain. He drew a blank, of course, as he'd expected.

There were no answers. They could play with him, like a cat juggling a mouse, letting him almost learn something—and then, always, they arrived just in time to prevent his success!

Put a rat in a maze where it can't learn the path, and it goes insane. But what good would he be to anyone if they drove him insane? And why bother with all that when they could silence him as well by killing him?

LESTER DEL REY

He'd forgotten to watch, and was surprised to find his feet on the steps of the apartment building. He jerked back, and bumped into someone.

"Sorry." The words came from behind him, automatically, and he turned to see the slim young man stepping aside. For a second, their eyes met squarely. A row of teeth flashed in a brief smile as the man started around him. "Guess I was thinking. Should have watched where I was going."

The man went on down the street, and turned in at the restaurant entrance.

*

Hawkes lifted a foot that weighed a ton and slowly closed his mouth. He'd been facing away from the street light—and his face might have been hard to see. Yet....

It didn't fit. The young man must have known him!

He blanked it from his mind. He couldn't believe that it was anything but lack of recognition. It was hard to see here, where the other was facing the light, and he was in the shadow.

But it still meant that they were waiting, nearby.

He dashed up the stairs, expecting a rush at both landings. The normal sounds of the apartment house went on. He listened at his door, but he could hear nothing except the same drip he had heard before. Slowly, he inserted the key and went in. The small bulb was still on. He crept along, trying to move silently on floors that insisted on creaking. The living room was as he had left it, and he caught sight of Ellen on the bed.

He spotted a mirror over one of the dressers, and used that to study more of the bedroom. It seemed as empty as before.

Finally, he stepped inside. There was no one there but Ellen, and she seemed to be asleep, doubled up in a position that might have made the unkind cords easier to stand. She moaned slightly as he untied her gently, but didn't awaken. Her breathing was regular, and

PURSUIT

her breath had the odd muskiness of someone who has slept for several hours.

He found a bottle of liquor on the shelf where she had put it, and rinsed out a couple of glasses. It was good liquor—good enough to take without mixers, as they'd have to do.

She came awake when he called her, rubbing her eyes and then her wrists, where the cords had left a mark. But she was smiling. "Hi, Will. I knew you'd come back. Hey, not on an empty stomach."

"You need it—and so do I," he told her. "Bottoms up!"

They were big glasses. She gasped over it, but she downed it, then reached for the water he had brought as a chaser. She swallowed, and blinked tears out of her eyes. "I don't usually drink."

He made no comment, but refilled the glass. The liquor had less effect on him than he'd expected, though he'd always had a good head for it. It took some of the edge off his worrying, though.

She giggled suddenly, and he frowned. She couldn't take much on an empty stomach, it seemed. Then he shrugged. Let her drink—maybe if he could get her drunk, he could find something out; at least he might learn whether the slim young man had been there during the day.

"Like when you found your dad's cider," she said, and giggled again. "You got awful—hp!—awful drunk, Willy, din't you? You were—so—funny!"

She was trying to be careful with her words already. She slid around, doing things that brought more honestly beautiful thigh into the light than Will had seen in ten years. He reached to adjust her dress, and she giggled again, sliding against him.

"You kissed me then, Willy. Remember? Bet you don' remember!"

*

He began it coldly, deliberately. If he could work on her emotions enough, he'd crack the wall of evasion and lies, somehow. He reached for her, calculating what would arouse her without causing any shock to bring her back to her senses.

LESTER DEL REY

He hadn't counted on the quickness of her reponse, nor the complete acceptance of his right with which she took it. The liquor had reduced her to the stage of a little girl who competely trusted her companion. She seemed as unconscious of her body as a child might be.

Instead of protesting, she reached down and began unfastening the buttons on her dress. "'Syour turn now, Willy. Put you to bed last night, you put me to bed t'-night. Then you gotta kiss me good-night. Nighty-night, nighty-night."

He felt like a heel at first. And then he began to feel like a man—any man around a beautiful girl half-undressed, and getting more so.

She slipped under the sheets, tossing out the last of her clothing, and crooning happily. "Gotta kiss me good-night, Willy. Nighty-night!"

He yanked the pull-cord savagely, cutting off the light, and fumbling in the darkness. After what seemed hours of awkwardness, he slid in beside her, feeling her arms go around him in complete acceptance. To hell with *them*! They could chase him some other time!

He pulled her to him, while his blood beat in his neck, and he began to lose any conscious volition of what he was doing. He drew her tighter, while a great clot of emotion set fire to his brain. He—

Cold beyond anything he had known bit at him. A tremendous pressure within him seemed about to force him to explode outwards, and the shock jerked him into full awareness.

In a split second, he swung his eyes from the great, jagged landscape on which he stood, up an impossible range of mountains that were all harsh blacks and cold whites, to a cold black sky in which the stars were blazing specks without a flicker. He saw the Earth above him, bigger than the moon had ever been, and with the dim outlines of continents showing through the soft stuff that must be clouds.

He was on the moon! And naked, without air!

PURSUIT

*

Almost at once, something clapped down around him, and the pressure let up, while heat seemed to leap into the rocks under his feet and make them comfortable. He gulped down the air that somehow seemed to stay close to him, instead of evaporating into the vacuum.

The moon! Now they had him!

Fear blazed in him—a stark, unreasoning terror that was like a physical thing. *Run—but you can't run! They've got you! You can't escape!*

The light blotted out, and then snapped on, more strongly. He stood in the kitchen of the cold-water apartment, still naked, with bits of chalky dust between his toes.

He had no time for reason. His brain seemed to have jumped over a hurdle and come down in a puddle beyond, foul with the stuff it had found there. He heard Ellen shriek, and then cry out again.

He lurched into the bedroom, while she let out another gurgling cry as the light showed him in the doorway. She came out of the bed, leaping for him, crying his name—cold sober! But he wanted none of her act. He shook her off.

"You damned alien! You filthy monster, disguised as a girl! When you get in a spot where I'm sure to find you out, you have a cute trick up your sleeve—but it won't work. You can send me back there—back to the rest of your kind, from wherever they came. But you won't fool me into thinking you're human again. You can't pass one test!"

He wouldn't be fooled into thinking it was a dream, either. He'd been physically on the moon—the very dust on his feet proved that. They might drive him insane, but they wouldn't do it that way.

She was crying now, gasping out words that he only half heard. "I'm human, Will. Oh, I'm human!"

"Then prove it! Come here, and prove it!"

She cried again at that, as he pulled her down with him. But slowly her crying quieted.

LESTER DEL REY

He awoke slowly, with sun-light streaming in the windows, and reached for her. He owed her more apologies than one, though he wasn't too sorry about most of it. She had proven herself human. And virginally so. Her complete surrender still left something warm inside him, where only the madness and the fear had been before.

Then he jerked upright, as he found her gone. He cursed himself for a fool, and listened for a stir and bustle from the kitchen, but there was none.

*

He was getting used to dressing with a feeling of dire pressure driving him on. He finished rapidly, and yanked the bedroom door open, just as he heard the outer lock click. She was coming in with a bottle of cream and a package of sausage as he reached the kitchen, and there was a smile tucked into the corner of her mouth.

And this time, he knew she wouldn't have betrayed him. Yet the fear increased in him. He darted past her as she leaned to kiss him, heading for the door. The room seemed to quiver. The hall was filled with a faint golden haze!

He had to get out! He jerked backwards, caught her hand, and pulled her. "Ellen! We've got to get out!"

It was a half-articulate shout, and she resisted, but he began dragging her after him. Something fumbled at the lock, and a key slipped into it. The door opened.

Hawkes didn't know what kind of an alien he expected. He knew that men could never have thrown him to the moon and back, not in another thousand years. It had to be a monster.

But he should have known that monsters here came in human form—they'd have to.

The fear rose to a shriek in his brain, and then died down as the human form entered. It was too normal—too familiar. A medium-sized man, dressed in a suit as inconspicuous as his own, wearing a silly little mustache that no outland monster should ever wear.

PURSUIT

The creature jumped in, slamming the door behind it. "Stay there! You can't risk it outside now! We've got to—"

Hawkes hit the figure with his shoulder, in the best football fashion he could muster. It could try—but it couldn't keep him and Ellen here to be burned in their heat-ray bath, or treated to whatever alien torture they had in mind. He felt his shoulder hit. And he knew he'd missed. It was an arm that he struck against, and the arm brought him upright, while a second arm drew back and came forward with a savage right to his jaw.

He went out with a dull plopping sound in his brain. Then, slowly, an ache came out of the blackness, and the beginning of sound. He was fighting out of the unconsciousness, fighting against time and the monster who'd try to steal Ellen.

But Ellen's hands were on his head, and an ice-cold towel was wet against his forehead. "Will! Will!"

*

He groaned and sat up. The other—alien or human—was gone.

"Where—?" he began.

She was trying to help him to his feet, and he got up groggily, with his head beginning to clear.

"He just ran out, Will." Ellen was crying, this time almost silently, with the words coming out between shakes of her shoulders. "Will, we've got to get out. We've got to. The men are coming for you. They'll be here any minute. And it's wrong—it won't work! Oh, Will, hurry!"

"Men? Men are coming?" He'd almost forgotten that it could be men who were after him.

"I called them, Will. I thought I had to. But it won't work. Will, do anything you like, but *get* out! They are fools. They...."

He opened the door and peered out the doorway into the hall, which seemed quiet. He'd been a fool again. He'd trusted her for some reason, as if a body and loyalty had to go together. They'd been smart, picking a virgin for the job. It must have cost them plenty, unless they'd twisted her mind somehow. Maybe they could do it.

But he knew that whatever they looked like, it couldn't be real men who'd meet him out there.

"Why?" he asked, and was surprised at the flatness of his voice.

She shook her head. "Because I'm a fool, Will. Because I thought they could help you—until *he* came! And because I'm still in love with you, even if you'd forgotten me."

But the fear inside him was drowning out her words, and the golden haze was faint in the air again.

"Okay," he said finally. "Okay, don't burn her, too, now that she's done your dirty work. I'm coming."

The haze disappeared slowly, and he started down the stairs, still holding her hand.

VI

here were men with guns in the street. He'd heard two shots as he came down the stairs, and had shoved Ellen behind him. But it was silent now. People with dazed, frightened faces were still darting into the houses, leaving the street to the men with the guns.

Hawkes marched forward grimly, perversely stripped of fear, even though he was sure some of the men out there were monsters and others were their dupes. He tapped one of the men on the shoulder.

"Okay, here I am. The girl goes free!"

The man spun around as if mounted on a ball bearing and pulled by strings. The gun fell from his hands. His emotion-taut face loosened suddenly, seemed to run like melted wax, and congealed again in an expression of utter idiocy. He gargled frothily, and then screamed—high and shrill, like a tortured woman.

Suddenly he was a lunging maniac, tearing up the street.

PURSUIT

Now the others were running—some toward cars, and some toward the corners, running flat and desperately on the flat of their feet, without any spring to their motions.

Hawkes jerked his eyes down toward the big gas-storage tanks where most of them had been, and the glow that had been in the corner of his vision was gone. Men seemed to be coming out of a trance. They were breaking away, forgetting about their guns and fleeing.

Three men alone were left.

Hawkes ducked back into the hall of the apartment, dragging Ellen with him. The glass of the door was somewhat dirty, but it made a dim mirror. He could see the slim young man and two others still there. The two men darted into a waiting car, and the leader turned up the street, running smoothly toward the apartment house.

Hawkes could make no sense of it—unless it was another of the seeming tricks designed to drive him out of his mind. He had decided he was one of the rats in the maze that didn't go crazy—the pressure could drive him somewhat mad, but it couldn't keep him that way.

He didn't wait to see what had happened, or whether the sirens that were sounding now were reinforcements for the men with guns or the police. He didn't bother with the slim young man any more. They'd apparently used their dupes to frighten out the people, and then had scared off the dupes—the poor humans who didn't know what it was all about. Now two of the three were gone, and the third monster was coming for him.

He'd escaped before. But sooner or later, they'd catch him—once they were sure he wouldn't be driven insane.

Or was this the beginning of insanity—a delusion of power, a feeling that he could escape? He could never know, if it was. He had to assume that he was sane.

*

He crouched back behind the stairs, while the young man in the gray tweeds dashed up them. Then he headed out into the street. The siren was near now—and tardily, he realized that the siren might

LESTER DEL REY

herald the coming of the real monsters. It was as easy to look like a cop as any other human!

He jerked open the door of the nearest car, pulled Ellen in, and kicked the motor to life. He gunned away from the curb, tossed it into second, and twisted around the corner, straight toward the siren that was nearest. At the last minute, he jerked to the side of the street, to let the police car shoot by. "Never run from a tiger—run toward it. It sometimes works, and it's no worse."

The car was a big one, and the motor purred smoothly. He glanced down at the dash, and frowned. There was no key in the switch. For a second, he stared at it, and then grinned. He'd picked a monster's car, apparently—they'd done a neat job of duplicating, but they didn't need all the safeguards that humans used, and the switch had obviously been a dummy.

He looked at the buttons on the dash, wondering which would make it levitate. But he had no desire to test it, nor to stay in an auto which could probably be traced so easily.

He braked to a halt outside the subway and led Ellen down.

"We're down to the last hole," he told her as the train pulled out of the station. "How much money do you have?"

She shook her head, and held up her arm. "I left it, Will."

They were beyond the last hole, then. He realized now that as long as they'd been in a crowded apartment house, filled with other humans, it had proved a tough nut to crack for the aliens. But on the move....

"Maybe we have a chance," he told her. "If humans were after me, it'd be tough—but these things have to avoid the police."

She looked at him, misery on her face. "There are no aliens, Will. Those men you saw were F. B. I. men. That's where I reported you."

"You...."

He stared at her, but she was serious.

"But there was nothing about me in the papers, Ellen."

PURSUIT

She pointed across the aisle. Spread over two columns on the front page, an older picture of him showed plainly. And even at the distance, the heading was boldly legible.

$100,000 REWARD FOR
THIS MAN!

He stared at the figure twice, unbelieving. He was no longer alone against a small group of humans or aliens. Now every living human on the face of the planet would be looking for him!

*

He could feel their hot breath on his neck, feel eyes staring at him through the papers. Fear began to rise in him, to be halted as the train ground to a new station. Ellen jerked him out, and he moved with her. It wasn't safe to be too long with one group, until they began to wonder and compare faces!

"But what—"

She shook her head. "Nothing, Will. I don't know. What can we do?"

He'd been wondering, while they moved quietly through the groups of people, and up the stairs. There was no place left. He had about a dollar in change, and that would be of no use to them. They'd have to dig a hole in the ground and pull it over them....

It joggled his memory, and he grabbed her hand and jerked open the door of a cab that was waiting for the light. He barked out an address——the corner of Tenth Avenue and one of the streets below Twentieth. The driver got into motion, not bothering to look back. The address was near enough to where Hawkes wanted to be—an old warehouse, with a loading platform. He'd played there as a kid, climbing back under it and digging holes down into the damp, soft earth, as kids have always done. He'd been by there since, and it had remained unchanged.

Sooner or later, the aliens would locate them. But it would give Ellen and him a chance to rest—perhaps long enough for him to

LESTER DEL REY

waylay someone at night and steal enough for them to leave town. That wouldn't be much help—but it was all he had left to count on.

He saw trucks loading there, as he paid the cab-driver. His heart sank abruptly, until he studied the way the big trailer was parked. If he watched carefully, he could slip under it from the side, and there was a chance he wouldn't be seen.

He darted beneath it.

Luck, for once was with him as he drew Ellen under the trailer and the platform. The old opening was covered with rubble, but he scraped it aside, and found an entrance barely big enough for them to wiggle through. Then they were back in a dark pocket under the back of the platform, barely big enough for them to sit upright. The hole had seemed bigger when he was a kid.

Outside, he heard a boy's voice yelling. "Monster attacks cops! Monster kills five cops! Extra Paper!"

Now he was a monster, to be shot on sight, probably.

"I shouldn't have brought you into this, Ellen," he said bitterly. "I should have left you. You don't even know what's going on—you haven't the faintest idea. If it were just humans, as you think...."

She snuggled against him in the coldness of the little cave. "Shh. I got you into it. I—I ratted on you, Scarface!"

*

But he couldn't reply to her attempt at humor. There was no fear now—not even the relief of fear. He'd felt brave for a few minutes, back in the hallway of the apartment. Now the chips were down, and sunk. They were here, in a dank hole, without food, and without a chance, while all the world searched for him to kill him—and while still-unknown aliens with unknown reasons played out their little game with consummate skill that would inevitably locate him.

It might take them a day—they probably would do nothing to him until night came, and the warehouse street was deserted! Ten more hours!

PURSUIT

If he only knew what they wanted of him, or why! If he could remember!

He sat there, numbed within himself. Ellen leaned her head forward onto his lap, and he began stroking her hair softly. He'd have liked to have had a chance with her. One night wasn't enough for a whole life. He reached down to draw her face to his....

Fear hit him, as something rustled behind him. He tried to turn and look, but his neck refused. The fear grew to panic, and swelled higher as the golden haze began to spread over the little cave. Then his muscles snapped his head around sharply. The slim young man was crawling toward them, holding something that looked like a flashlight. Behind it, he could see the tense lips drawn back over clenched teeth. The man wasn't smiling now. He opened his mouth, just as the thing like a flashlight sprang into light.

No time seemed to elapse, but suddenly Ellen and the young man were both gone, and he sat in the dark hole, alone. He let out an animal cry, and dashed out, crawling through the opening, and kicking the rubble back as he went. He slipped out, and under the trailer. But there was no sign. They'd taken her, and left him unconscious!

He groaned, trying to figure. He'd always gone back to the same place to hide, since he'd found it. They must expect him back there. They'd take Ellen there and wait for him, drugging her, changing her mind, setting her up to use against him. The first time hadn't worked, but they'd try it again. It had to be that. If they hadn't taken her there, he had no way of finding her, and he had to find her.

He began running down the street, forcing himself to believe she was there. Then he slowed. It would do no good to have them all notice him, here on the street. Someone might recognize him then. He turned around, walking back to the bus stop. There were still two dimes and a nickel in his pocket.

*

LESTER DEL REY

He hunched down on the seat of the bus that seemed to crawl up Tenth Avenue. But no one noticed him in the almost empty vehicle. He got off at Sixty-Sixth and forced himself to walk to West End, up that to the apartment-house.

Men were drawing up in cars—men with guns in their hands. He made a final dash for the apartment entrance. This must be the real show—for which the other had been only a dress rehearsal to throw him off balance. They could wait.

He fumbled with the lock, until he finally got it open. Then he jumped in, slamming the door shut behind him. Ellen stood there, and the creature that had assaulted him before was pawing at her. But he had no time for the monster.

"Stay there!" he shouted at her. "You can't risk it outside now! We've got to—"

He saw she wasn't listening to him. He had to get rid of the creature somehow, if he could get it far enough away from her. Then they'd find some way to get outside, without going out through the entrance.

The creature sprang at him awkwardly. His arm darted down to catch one shoulder, and his right hand swung back and up. There was a savage satisfaction in seeing the creature crumple.

Ellen's voice reached him. "Will! Will, before I go crazy...."

"You're free," he told her. "Go down the fire escape and leave that here. I'll get rid of them out front somehow."

He shut the door again, and went down. The words had sounded brave enough, but there had been no courage behind them. Fear still rode him, like the little golden haze that again hovered over him, showing they had spotted him.

He walked out, with it thick around him, rising slowly in temperature. They had him—but Ellen might get away. He walked down the steps, his hands up. They drew back, surprise and something else on their features, their eyes on the haze that surrounded him. They were shouting, but he couldn't hear the words

PURSUIT

over the shrieks of the people along the street, rushing inside or trying to drag their kids to safety.

Hawkes doubled his legs under him and leaped. He was still attacking the tiger—the slim young man, down by the big gas-storage tanks, directing the new crop of human dupes.

His charge carried him there, while the young man slipped aside. Then someone fired a gun.

He heard the young man yell hoarsely. "No shooting! Stop it! Damn it, NO SHOOTING!"

They weren't paying any attention to the shouts. Bullets ticked against the tanks. Hawkes ducked frantically, physical fear knotting his stomach.

*

Suddenly, he seemed to jerk upwards, to find himself suspended in mid-air, fifty feet off the ground, just beyond the tanks. He stared down at the men, dizzy with the height, but no longer surprised by anything. The men were pointing their guns upwards, while the young man leaped about among them. Bullets were splatting out, though none came near Hawkes. They seemed to ricochet off the air a few feet in front of him.

The slim young man drew back. And now, the rubble and stones along the street began to lift, and to drive savagely at the attackers. A gale swept along the street, though Hawkes could feel no breath of air, and the force of it was enough to knock most of them down.

They got up and began running, dashing away from the super-science that the young man now seemed bent on turning against his own troop of dupes, now that they were out of control.

Hawkes came drifting downward. He started to cry out in fear, until he noticed that the ground was coming up at him slowly, and that he was slipping sideways. He landed on a street back of the tanks, as gently as a feather.

Surprisingly, everyone was gone when he risked a glance back at the scene of the fight, with the back of the slim man just darting into the apartment house. Then Hawkes cursed, as the creature came darting out, with Ellen behind him, to leap into a car and drive off. The sound of sirens grew louder, and a police car swung onto West End.

Hawkes straightened up slowly, as it hit him. It had been the same scene he'd gone through before that morning—but with himself in the middle! He shot a glance at the sun, to see it still to the east, though his memory of the day indicated it should have been after noon.

Time! They'd twisted him back through time—the weapon that had looked like a flashlight must have tossed him hours backwards, instead of knocking him out. He'd been attacking himself there in the hallway of his apartment! He'd knocked himself out. And the fight he had just been through was the same fight that he had seen come to its end before!

Now, his younger self and Ellen must be just fleeing toward the hideout under the loading platform, with the slim man still following. If he could get there in time, before the man could run off with Ellen....

VII

he paper he'd found kept the other passengers on the bus from seeing him, but he was too deep in his own thoughts to read it. His eyes roamed back to the story of the cop-killing monster—a seemingly harmless florist in Brooklyn who'd suddenly gone berserk and rushed down the streets with a knife; he'd been wrong in thinking that concerned him. And he'd been wrong in thinking anyone would try to kill him on sight. The reward notice and picture were in front of his eyes—but it was a reward for information, and there was a huge box that proclaimed he was *not* a criminal and must not be harmed, or even allowed to know he was recognized.

The new facts only confused the issue. He twisted about in his mind, trying to explain why the young man had left him to drift

PURSUIT

down, and gone rushing into the apartment. He was ready for the collecting—and he'd been left uncollected!

The girl had said there were no aliens. Now he wondered. She had known more than he'd found from her—she'd known his brand of cigarettes, even. And there had been that shopping list, with the lipstick on it—the same type he now remembered her using. He'd known her before—and not just as a little girl. That tied him in with Meinzer, who was a mystery in himself.

He puzzled over it. The things that had happened to him had always been preceded by violent emotion, instead of followed by it. Usually, it had been fear—but sometimes some other emotion, as had been the case just before he was suddenly shifted to the Moon. Whenever he seemed on the verge of discovering something or emotionally upset, it hit at him. Did that mean he was only susceptible to the phenomena when off balance? It still didn't account for the fact that some of the things hadn't directly affected him, at all.

The more he knew, the less he knew.

He got off the bus and headed for the warehouse. This time, he had to wait before he could see a chance to dart under the trailer and into the entrance. He noticed that the gray sedan was parked nearby.

He darted in.

They were still there! He heard Ellen's voice, sounding as if she had been crying, and then an answer from the other. He felt his way carefully over the rubble, working as close as he could. Now, if he sprang the few feet....

"... must be a time-jump," the man's voice said, doubtfully. "I tell you, Ellen, those damned fools were firing at him, up there in the air, while you were still with him in the apartment. That's an angle on this psi factor stuff we hadn't expected."

The voice stopped for a moment. Then it picked up again. "Drat it! I wish you hadn't called the F. B. I. on him—they got rattled when he came out looking like a saint in a halo and jumped fifty feet up to float around. Some fool started shooting, and the rest joined in."

"I had to—he was talking about alien monsters. I thought he was going crazy, Dan. I couldn't tell him anything—I promised him I wouldn't, and I kept my promise. But I thought enough of them might catch him, somehow.... Dan, can't we find him now? He needs us!"

*

Hawkes lay frozen. He tried to move forward, but his body was tensed, waiting for more. If something happened now....

"Alien monsters?" Dan's voice grew bitter. "It is alien—and a monster. This psi factor...."

The words blurred, and seemed to echo and re-echo inside Hawkes' head. That made twice he'd heard them mention the psi factor—the strange ability a few human minds had to perform seeming miracles. Men who had it could make dice roll the way they wanted. Young girls sometimes had it before puberty, and could throw heavy objects around a room without touching them; they did not even know they were the cause of the motion, but blamed it on poltergeists. Other men caused strange accidents—fires, for instance—the old salamander legend!

There'd been a piece of paper—psi equals alpha, the psi factor was the beginning of infinity for mankind. But it had been wrong. He'd changed that, on the other side. It should have read psi equals omega, the absolute end.

He gasped hoarsely, and heard their startled voices stop, while the flashlight beam swung around, to pick him out in the darkness. He felt Ellen and her younger brother, Dan, pulling him forward into the little cave with them, and he heard their voices questioning him. But his head was spinning madly under the sudden flood of memories that the missing key word had suddenly brought back.

The letter from Professor Meinzer had been about his paper on poltergeists which the old man had seen before publication. He'd

PURSUIT

been doing research on the psi factor for the government, and he needed a mathematician—even one who proved something which he knew wasn't true, provided the mathematics could handle his theories.

Hawkes' head was suddenly brimming with mental images of the seven months, while he worked on the mathematics to tie down the strange pattern of brain waves the old professor had found in the minds of those who had the mysterious psi factor. Dan had worked with them, in the little cluttered apartment, building the apparatus they needed. It was through Dan that Ellen was hired, as a general assistant and secretary.

There had been only the four of them, working in deepest secrecy in the three rooms which the government had felt were more suitable to maintain complete security than any deeply buried laboratory could have been. Ellen made a pretense of living there, and it was a neighborhood where no landlady worried about the men who went to a girl's place, provided everything was quiet.

They'd succeeded, too—they had found the tiny bundle of cells that controlled the psi factor, and learned to stimulate them by artificial wave trains and hypnosis. But the small group in the top division of the government to whom they were responsible had demanded more proof.

*

Hawkes had treated himself secretly, not knowing that Meinzer had done the same two days before. And both had learned the same thing. The wild talents appeared, but they couldn't be controlled. Meinzer hadn't found security in the hospital, hard as he'd tried to find it. He'd gotten up in the middle of the night and walked through the solid wall, unable to stop until he was back with the group.

Hawkes had tried another way to stop the wild abilities that operated without his conscious control. He'd prepared a new hypnotic tape, worded to make him forget everything he knew, or even the fact that he had worked on the psi factor. He'd put in commands that would make him avoid any reference to it, so that he couldn't learn accidentally. He'd ordered his brain to have nothing to do with it. Then he'd drugged himself with a combination of opiates and hypnotics that should have knocked out a horse. Then he'd telephoned Dan to have men pick him up in an hour and keep him drugged. He'd turned on the tape recorder and stumbled back to the bed.

He groaned, as he remembered his failure. "It's the ultimate, absolute alien, all right—the back of a man's own mind. It's Freud's unconsciousness, or id. The psi factor is controlled by that, and not by the conscious mind. And the id is a primitive beast—it operates on raw impulse, without reason or social consciousness. Every man's unconsciousness is back in the jungle, before civilization—and we've given that alien thing the greatest power that could exist when we wake up the psi power."

"Meinzer thought it was controlled, for a while," Ellen said. "He came when Dan and I called him. I went with him up to your apartment, while Dan got the men to carry you away. But we couldn't reach you—Meinzer barely touched the tape-recorder when something seemed to pick us up and drive us out of the room and down the stairs. We were just going back when you came out."

She shuddered, and Hawkes nodded. He'd obviously used that psi factor to throw off the drugs at the first sign of anyone near him. He told them sickly what had happened to the old man.

"So I killed him," he finished bitterly.

Dan shook his head. "No. Your psi factor works differently. You control heat and radiation, you can move yourself or any object in space for almost any distance, instantly if you want, and it seems you can do the same through time. But you can't disintegrate things, as Meinzer could. He had a suicide urge—we knew that before. When it got out of control again, he blew himself up—just as your dominant urge to protect yourself did all those things around you."

PURSUIT

*

Hawkes grimaced. It wasn't pleasant to know, that he'd been doing all the things he'd blamed on monsters. He'd somehow remembered that someone was supposed to come to get him, and he'd run out in wild fear, while his unconscious mind blasted the apartment with heat to destroy all traces. He'd blasted down the subway entrance with another bolt of energy to make his getaway. The poor cat had surprised him, and been killed. His unconsciousness gone wild had tossed Dan's car two hundred feet to the roof of the garage. When it found him losing control emotionally with Ellen, it hadn't let his conscious brain give it the information it needed—it had simply thrown him completely off Earth, pulled air to him, and warmed the rocks. Then, when it found the Moon unfit for life, it had thrown him back to his own world. It had tossed him hours back in time this morning, and lifted him into the air while it pelted his "enemies" with rocks, and built a wall around him by throwing the bullets back instantly.

And it had somehow clung to the implanted idea that he must not find out about himself. It had destroyed anything where the written word might give him a hint, and had even melted the telephone so that he couldn't continue listening to other evidence.

It had probably done a thousand other things that he couldn't even remember, whenever its wild, reasonless fears were aroused and it decided that he had to be protected!

"You should have killed me," he told them. But he knew that they couldn't have done it.

"We had to let you sweat it out. You made us promise not to tell you anything, and we thought you might be right," Ellen told him. "We thought that it might adjust after awhile. All we did was to try to pick you up, until we knew it was impossible."

"Until Sis tipped off the Government men," Dan added. Hawkes could imagine what their reaction had been to having a man with his power running wild. He was surprised that they had bothered to make even an attempt to see that he wasn't harmed.

He shrugged helplessly. "And where does it leave us now—beyond this hole in the ground?"

"The Government's put about fifty specialists on the notes you and Meinzer left," Dan answered, but there was no assurance in his voice. "They're trying to find some way to bring the psi factor under the control of your logical, rational mind."

He got to his knees and began crawling out of the little cave, while Hawkes tried to help Ellen follow him. Outside, Dan knocked off the dirt from his clothes and headed for the sedan he'd, somehow gotten off the roof.

Hawkes followed, for want of anything better to do.

He knew the answers now—and he was worse off than ever. Instead of a horde of outside aliens, he had one single monster in his own skull, where he could never fight it, or even hope to escape it.

The power had been meant as a hope for the world. A man who could work such seeming miracles might have ended the threat of war; he'd have been the perfect spy, or better at attack than a hundred hydrogen bombs that had to smash whole cities to remove a few men and weapons. But now the world was better off without him. So long as he still lived, there would be nothing but danger from the alien monster in his head. He had no idea of his limits—but he was sure that it could trigger the energies of the universe to move the whole world out of its orbit, if that seemed necessary for his personal survival!

VIII

Hawkes leaned forward cautiously as the gray sedan moved up Tenth Avenue. His finger found the gun in Dan's coat pocket; and he pulled it out stealthily.

He knew that the only answer for him was suicide. He had to destroy himself, since no one else could!

PURSUIT

He propped it up, pointing at his head, and his thumb pressed back on the trigger, further and further, until he felt sure the smallest change would set it off. Then he waited for the rough spot in the street or the sudden stop at a light that would do the trick before he could stop it.

The car lurched—and the gun suddenly vanished, leaving his hand empty.

His responses were too quick—and his mind wasn't waiting, once it knew there was danger. He slumped back on the rear seat, trying to think. Drugs were out—he knew his system could throw them off.

But he couldn't remove himself!

He lifted his wrist—to his teeth, and bit down savagely. If he could sever an artery.... Pain shot through him, and he stared down at the blood.

Then the blood was gone, and the wound was closing before his eyes, until only smooth flesh remained. His mind could juggle the cells back into their original form.

It would have to be sudden, complete death.

And no death was that sudden! For a fraction of a second, there'd be life left—and during that split second, the damage would be repaired, or he would be shifted from danger.

There was no way out—unless he could pull himself to another planet, or throw himself back into the dim past. But that would take voluntary control, and he knew now that hours of effort had shown him how impossible that was. He hadn't been able to lift a crumb of bread from the table deliberately, in his original tests after he had treated himself.

He was faced with a problem that had to be solved—and there was no possible solution that he could find.

No man could face that dilemma forever without going insane. Hawkes shuddered, trying to picture what would happen if he went mad, and the wild talents began operating at every whim of his crazed mind!

LESTER DEL REY

*

Ellen shouted suddenly, grabbing for the wheel. Hawkes felt himself tense, and began lifting from the seat of the car. But there was no visible danger, and Dan was slowing to a halt at the curb, Hawkes' body dropped back slowly.

"Dan," Ellen was whispering hoarsely. "Dan, we can't. If we take him back, they'll find him, and they'll know what he can do. They'll kill him. Eventually, they'll kill Will!"

Hawkes started to protest, but Dan's words cut him short.

"You're right, Sis. They'll wait their time, until he won't know when to expect it—and then they'll drop an H-bomb on him, if they have to. That's faster than any nerve impulse!"

He swung back to face Hawkes, reaching for the door of the car. "Get out, Will—and get as far away as you can. I'm not going to drive you to your death. They'll get you eventually, but I won't be the one to make it easier for them!"

Hawkes jerked. The old fear came back suddenly.

You can't escape! They'll get you. Run! GO!

He screamed, as the golden haze flickered again. He could wipe out the Earth, but he couldn't survive, then. He could move back in time, but it would only mean other dangers—no man could stay awake forever, and he was used to civilized living.

The haze hesitated, while the sense of danger mounted. Then it was gone, as if the beast in his head had found no answer.

Suddenly the gray sedan lifted again, to a height of fifty feet above the tallest building. It shot forward, hesitated, and came down softly on a deserted side-road in Central Park.

His mind felt as if it were going to split. Dan and Ellen stared at him speechlessly.

You can't survive alone! No power is enough by itself! They'll get you! You are your own death-sentence! RUN! DON'T RUN!

PURSUIT

Hawkes put his hand to his splitting skull, trying to force words through the agonies of pain, while slow understanding began to reach him.

"Dan! The scientists ... get me there!"

Then his mind seemed to clamp down on itself, and he was unconscious. He could protect himself from almost anything—except his own brain!

*

He was conscious of no pain, but only of irritation. There was a needle in his arm, and he removed it!

He opened his eyes slowly, to find himself the center of a group of men, while a white-clothed doctor stood staring at an empty hand that must have held a hypodermic.

Ellen cried out suddenly, and ran to him, cradling his head in her hands. He found her arm with his own hand, and stroked it slowly.

"You've found the answer?" he asked. Then he nodded, while the weight that had lain on him so long began to lift. His voice was suddenly positive. "You found it!"

One of the men pushed forward, but Dan shook his head, and came over to stand beside the cot where Hawkes lay. "No, Will. They didn't find it—you did! You found what we should have known—your unconscious mind may be a wild beast, but it isn't insane. When it was shocked into realizing that it couldn't save you by itself, it looked for help from your consciousness. And then it knocked you out—knocked itself out—until we could work on you."

"I guessed it," Hawkes said slowly. "But in that case, a psychotic with his id out in the driver's seat should become normal when they lock him up. Or wait—maybe his unconsciousness is a bit insane. Maybe. But you still have to communicate with that unconscious part of the brain, to make it understand that it has to surrender. And all the psychiatrists have been driving themselves crazy trying to solve that!"

LESTER DEL REY

"*Touché*," an older man said, and there was a faint sound of amusement from some of the others. "But this psi factor is the means of communication! You told us that yourself, while you were undergoing our hastily improvised hypnotic education of your brain. It always has been. The minute a girl bothered with poltergeists finds she is the cause of them, they stop. It's a faint, weak channel between consciousness and unconsciousness—or subconsciousness, if you prefer. And yours was widened by the treatment, even if it wasn't ready to work yet. We simply used your own technique to improve the relationship. All you ever needed was a longer, harder treatment than you and Meinzer had given yourselves. You just stopped too soon."

*

Hawkes dropped back comfortably onto the cot. He reached out for a glass of water, lifted it to his lips, and put it back—without using his hands. He thought of his clothes, and they were suddenly on him, over the single white garment he had been wearing. Another thought took that away, to leave him normally dressed.

Whether they were entirely correct or not in their theories, the psi factor was no longer wild. He had it under full control!

He sat up, just as three men entered the crowded room. One wore the uniform of a four-star general, but the familiar faces of the two civilians told Hawkes at once that they were more important than any general could be.

He was about to become officially the National Arsenal and replacement for all the armies, navies, and air-corps they had ever dreamed of having. He'd also become their bridge into space, their means of solving the secrets of the planets, and probably their chief historical tool, since nothing could ever be secret from him.

It was going to be a busy life for him and for the others like him who would now be carefully selected and treated!

He grinned faintly, as he realized that they didn't know yet just how important he was. He wasn't going to be a National

PURSUIT

Resource—he'd be a World Resource. This power was too great for any local political use, and no man who had it along with the full correlation of his conscious and subconscious mind could ever see it any other way.

But right now, he had other pressing business. He grinned at Ellen. "You don't mind a small wedding, do you?" he asked.

She shook her head, beginning to smile. He reached for her hand. This psi factor was going to be a handy thing to have around, with its complete control of space and time.

"I'm taking a two-week honeymoon before we talk business," he told the approaching three men. "But don't go away. We'll be back in ten minutes!"

Honolulu looked lovely in the moonlight, and June was the perfect month for a wedding.

*

EDITORIAL NOTE: Actually, *Pursuit* ends where the real story is just beginning! Disregarding other powers, when men can move instantly over any distance by simple desire, it's the beginning of a life and culture totally unrelated to anything we know. What will it be like? Where should houses be built—and will they be built? A housewife can have her dining-room in the mountains and her kitchen in a community (to simplify and cheapen plumbing, etc.) 10,000 miles away, or on another planet! There can be no national boundaries, of course. What happens to the multiplicity of languages? What happens to government? How do you catch a criminal? How do you hold him?

There are endless possibilities, naturally. We're tossing it open to the readers. You tell us what you think that world will be like—if you can! We'll print the best letters—and if the authors want to use this background, we'll buy the best stories based on it.

We will not be responsible for mental break-downs, however!

www.ingramcontent.com/pod-product-compliance
Lightning Source LLC
Chambersburg PA
CBHW031429040426
42444CB00006B/744